Informing the legislative debate since 1914 _____

The Post-9/11 Veterans Educational Assistance Act of 2008 (Post-9/11 GI Bill): Primer and Issues

Analyst in Education Policy

July 28, 2014

Congressional Research Service

7-5700

www.crs.gov

R42755

CRS REPORT
Prepared for Members and
Committees of Congress _____

Summary

The Post-9/11 Veterans Educational Assistance Act of 2008 (Post-9/11 GI Bill®)—enacted as Title V of the Supplemental Appropriations Act, 2008 (P.L. 110-252) on June 30, 2008—is the newest GI Bill and went into effect on August 1, 2009. There were four main drivers for the Post-9/11 GI Bill: (1) providing parity of benefits for reservists and members of the regular Armed Forces, (2) ensuring comprehensive educational benefits, (3) meeting military recruiting goals, and (4) improving military retention through transferability of benefits. By FY2010, the program had the largest numbers of participants and the highest total obligations compared to the other GI Bills.

The Post-9/11 GI Bill provides benefits to veterans and servicemembers who serve on active duty after September 10, 2001. Participants may be eligible for payments to cover tuition and fees, housing, books and supplies, tutorial and relocation assistance, and testing and certification fees. Individuals who serve on active duty for 36 months after September 10, 2001, may receive a tuition and fees benefit of up to the amount of in-state tuition and fees charged when enrolled in public institutions of higher learning (IHLs), or up to $19,198.31 when enrolled in private IHLs in academic year 2013-2014. Benefit payments vary depending on the participant's active duty status, length of qualifying active duty, rate of pursuit, and program of education.

There are two mechanisms by which dependents of individuals with military service may be eligible for Post-9/11 GI Bill benefits. Transferred Post-9/11 GI Bill benefits may be available to the dependents of servicemembers who stay in the military for at least 10 years. Also, the Post-9/11 GI Bill Marine Gunnery Sergeant John David Fry Scholarship Program may be available to the children of servicemembers who die while serving on active duty in the line of duty.

The Post-9/11 Veterans Educational Assistance Improvements Act of 2010 (P.L. 111-377) made several amendments to eligibility and benefits under the Post-9/11 GI Bill. The Restoring GI Bill Fairness Act of 2011 (P.L. 112-26) temporarily reversed a P.L. 111-377 amendment to the tuition and fees benefit for some individuals. The Honoring America's Veterans and Caring for Camp Lejeune Families Act of 2012 (P.L. 112-154) requires the Department of Defense (DOD) and Department of Veterans Affairs (VA) to provide annual reports to Congress on the Post-9/11 GI Bill and the Survivors' and Dependents' Educational Assistance program (DEA).

Congress, administrators, and participants have raised several issues recently. The 113th Congress has considered mechanisms to increase the benefit level for individuals who are not charged in-state tuition. Despite the Yellow Ribbon program, participants attending public IHLs out-of-state may incur considerable out-of-pocket cost. Another salient issue in light of the amount of federal funds devoted to these benefits, an average of $13,465 per participant and a total of $10.2 billion in FY2013, regards the quality of the programs of education for which Post-9/11 GI Bill participants use their benefits, the ability of participants to make informed decisions on the use of benefits, and misleading or deceptive recruiting techniques of some IHLs. The VA, in partnership with DOD and the Department of Education, is implementing Executive Order 13607, *Establishing Principles of Excellence for Educational Institutions Serving Service Members, Veterans, Spouses, and Other Family Members*, and the Improving Transparency of Education Opportunities for Veterans Act of 2012 (P.L. 112-249) to improve disclosures to and protections for Post-9/11 GI Bill participants. Issues have also been raised regarding benefit overpayments, transferability, benefit uses, and qualifying active duty service.

Contents

Tables

Contacts

Background

The newest veterans educational assistance program (GI Bill[®][1]) was enacted on June 30, 2008, as the Post-9/11 Veterans Educational Assistance Act of 2008 (Post-9/11 GI Bill), Title V of the Supplemental Appropriations Act, 2008 (P.L. 110-252). Congress found that "service on active duty in the Armed Forces [had] been especially arduous for the members of the Armed Forces since September 11, 2001," and that there was a need for an educational assistance program that provided "enhanced educational assistance benefits ... worthy of such service."[2] The benefits were designed to meet four main objectives: (1) provide parity of benefits for reservists and members of the regular Armed Forces, (2) ensure comprehensive educational benefits, (3) meet military recruiting goals, and (4) improve military retention through transferability of benefits. There was a desire for reservists to receive benefits equivalent to members of the regular Armed Forces for equivalent, though often not continuous, active duty service. It was recognized that veterans and servicemembers would be eligible for U.S. Department of Education (ED) student financial aid benefits such as Pell Grants and Stafford Loans;[3] U.S. Department of Defense (DOD) educational assistance; and various state, local, and other federal benefits in addition to the basic Post-9/11 GI Bill benefits. Members of Congress hoped that a benefit that exceeded that available under the other active GI Bills would ameliorate military recruiting challenges and reduce the higher unemployment rate among veterans compared with non-veterans of the same age group.[4]

There was some discussion about whether increasing the monthly benefit might result in lower retention in the Armed Forces. Some DOD research suggested that education is not a very important factor in the decision to stay in or leave the military, while other evidence suggested that very high benefits would encourage discharge. DOD considered the ability to transfer benefits to dependents critical to retention. The Administration was interested in transferability as well, and President George W. Bush advocated for transferability in a State of the Union address.[5]

The Post-9/11 GI Bill is codified under Title 38 U.S.C., Chapter 33. The stated purpose is to reward members of the Armed Forces for service on active duty since September 11, 2001;

---

[1] GI Bill[®] is a registered trademark of the United States Department of Veterans Affairs (VA).

[2] P.L. 110-252

[3] Title IV of the Higher Education Act of 1965, as amended, authorizes several student aid programs: Pell Grant program, William D. Ford Federal Direct Loan (DL) Program, American Competitiveness Grant program, National Science and Mathematics Access to Retain Talent (SMART) Grant program, Federal Supplemental Educational Opportunity Grant (FSEOG) program, Leveraging Educational Assistance Partnership (LEAP) program, Federal Work-Study (FWS) program, Federal Perkins Loan program, and Grants for Access and Persistence (GAP) program. See CRS Report R42446, *Federal Pell Grant Program of the Higher Education Act: How the Program Works, Recent Legislative Changes, and Current Issues*, by Shannon M. Mahan; CRS Report RL31618, *Campus-Based Student Financial Aid Programs Under the Higher Education Act*, by Alexandra Hegji and David P. Smole; and CRS Report R40122, *Federal Student Loans Made Under the Federal Family Education Loan Program and the William D. Ford Federal Direct Loan Program: Terms and Conditions for Borrowers*, by David P. Smole.

[4] U.S. Congress, House Committee on Veterans' Affairs, Subcommittee on Economic Opportunity, *Pending Montgomery GI Bill Legislation*, 110th Cong., 2nd sess., January 17, 2008, HRG-2008-VAH-0003 (Washington: GPO, 2008), pp. 3, 6, 9, 10, 14; and U.S. Congress, Senate Committee on Veterans' Affairs, *Hearing on Pending Benefits Legislation*, 110th Cong., 2nd sess., May 7, 2008, S. Hrg. 110-675 (Washington: GPO, 2008), pp. 15, 21, 34, 49.

[5] U.S. Congress, House Committee on Veterans' Affairs, Subcommittee on Economic Opportunity, *Pending Montgomery GI Bill Legislation*, 110th Cong., 2nd sess., January 17, 2008, HRG-2008-VAH-0003 (Washington: GPO, 2008), pp. 3, 6, 9, 10, 14; and U.S. Congress, Senate Committee on Veterans' Affairs, *Hearing on Pending Benefits Legislation*, 110th Cong., 2nd sess., May 7, 2008, S. Hrg. 110-675 (Washington: GPO, 2008), pp. 15, 21, 34, 49.

maintain a history of offering educational assistance to veterans; respond to the needs of the Armed Forces when not at peace; demonstrate the high esteem with which military service is held; recognize the difficult challenges involved in readjusting to civilian life after serving; and enhance the educational assistance benefits to those who serve on active duty after September 10, 2001. The Post-9/11 GI Bill provides aid payments to participants pursuing approved programs of education for tuition and fees, housing, books and supplies, and other education-related expenditures. The program became effective August 1, 2009. By FY2010, the program had the largest numbers of participants and the highest total obligations compared to the other GI Bills.[6] The program is permanently authorized and supported through mandatory funds.

Following enactment, concerns were raised about several aspects of the Post-9/11 GI Bill, and calls were made for the program to be amended. Several laws have been passed to amend programmatic aspects of the Post-9/11 GI Bill:

- The Supplemental Appropriations Act, 2009 (P.L. 111-32), enacted on June 24, 2009, created the Marine Gunnery Sergeant John David Fry Scholarship.

- The Post-9/11 Veterans Educational Assistance Improvements Act of 2010 (Improvements Act; P.L. 111-377), enacted on January 4, 2011, made several amendments to the Post-9/11 GI Bill and other veterans educational assistance programs.[7]

- The Restoring GI Bill Fairness Act of 2011 (P.L. 112-26), enacted on August 3, 2011, temporarily reverses one amendment of the Improvements Act for some individuals attending private institutions of higher learning (IHLs) in seven states.[8]

- The Honoring America's Veterans and Caring for Camp Lejeune Families Act of 2012 (P.L. 112-154), enacted on August 6, 2012, requires annual reports to Congress on the Post-9/11 GI Bill and the Survivors' and Dependents' Educational Assistance program (DEA; 38 U.S.C., Chapter 35).

- The National Defense Authorization Act for Fiscal Year 2013 (P.L. 112-239), enacted on January 2, 2013, expanded eligibility to certain members of the Coast Guard Reserve.

The amendments will be noted in this report, as applicable. Additional issues that have been raised and which might be addressed by Congress include the level of benefits, the quality of educational programs, and the administration of those benefits.

This report provides a detailed description of the Post-9/11 GI Bill and related issues. The first section describes the participant eligibility criteria. The second section indicates a participant's entitlement to benefits and the period during which the benefits must be used. The third section describes the eligible programs of education. The subsequent section explains the eligible benefit payments. This is followed by descriptions of the two Post-9/11 GI Bill provisions for

---

[6] For a description of the other GI Bills, see CRS Report R40723, *Educational Assistance Programs Administered by the U.S. Department of Veterans Affairs*, by Cassandria Dortch (available upon request).

[7] For a detailed description of the Improvements Act amendments, see CRS Report R41620, *The Post-9/11 Veterans Educational Assistance Improvements Act of 2010, As Enacted*, by Cassandria Dortch.

[8] Until passage of P.L. 112-26, some individuals in the seven states would have had larger out-of-pocket costs in academic year 2011-2012 than in the prior academic year, 2010-2011.

dependents—the Marine Gunnery Sergeant John David Fry Scholarship Program and the transferability option. The final sections illustrate key links to other programs administered by the U.S. Department of Veterans Affairs (VA), present data on obligations and participation, and portray key issues that may be addressed by Congress.

Eligible Individuals

Under the Post-9/11 GI Bill, veterans and servicemembers of the Army, Navy, Marine Corps, Air Force, and Coast Guard, including the reserve components, and commissioned officers of the Public Health Service (PHS) and the National Oceanic and Atmospheric Association (NOAA), may be eligible. Individuals must serve an aggregate minimum of 90 days on active duty after September 10, 2001, or individuals must have been discharged or released for a service-connected disability after serving a minimum of 30 continuous days on active duty after September 10, 2001. For the reserves, qualifying active duty means a call or order to active duty under Title 10 U.S.C. Sections 688, 12301(a), 12301(d), 12301(g), 12302, and 12304; full-time duty under Title 32;[9] and Title 14 U.S.C. Section 712.[10]

The active duty service period includes service on active duty in entry-level and skill training[11] if the total active duty service period is at least 24 months.[12] The Post-9/11 GI Bill qualifying active duty service period excludes time assigned to a civilian institution for an education or training program similar to those offered to civilians, excludes time spent as a cadet or midshipman at one of the service academies, excludes other active duty service periods required to meet a service academy or Reserve Officer Training Corps (ROTC) obligation, excludes service that is terminated because of a defective enlistment and induction, and excludes active duty service periods required to meet a student loan repayment obligation (10 U.S.C., Chapter 109).

Once the active duty service period is met, individuals must either continue on active duty or be discharged or released from active duty in one of the following manners:

- with an honorable discharge;

- with active duty characterized as honorable service and placement on the retired list, transfer to the Fleet Reserve or Fleet Marine Corps Reserve, or placement on the temporary disability retired list;

---

[9] The Post-9/11 Veterans Educational Assistance Improvements Act of 2010 (Improvements Act) expanded the qualifying active duty service periods to include full-time duty under a Title 32 call to order for National Guard members effective on August 1, 2009, and payable after September 30, 2011.

[10] The National Defense Authorization Act for Fiscal Year 2013 (P.L. 112-239) expanded the qualifying active duty service periods to include short-term, disaster response activation of the Coast Guard Reserve under Title 14 on or after December 31, 2011, to ensure parity between the Coast Guard Reserve and other reserves.

[11] Entry-level and skill training is defined as basic combat training, advanced individual training, and one station unit training (OSUT) in the Army; recruit training (or boot camp) and skill training (or so-called 'A' school) in the Navy; basic military training and technical training in the Air Force, recruit training and Marine Corps training (or school of infantry training) in the Marine Corps; and basic training and skill training (or so-called 'A' school) in the Coast Guard.

[12] If the period of active duty service including entry-level and skill training is at least 24 months but the period of active duty service excluding entry-level and skill training is less than 18 months, the applicable active duty period is 18 months.

- with active duty characterized as honorable service and further service in a reserve component; or

- with active duty characterized as honorable service as a result of a medical condition which preceded active duty and is not service-connected, a hardship, or a physical or mental condition that was not characterized as a disability and did not result from the individual's own willful misconduct but did interfere with the individual's performance of duty.[13]

Many Post-9/11 GI Bill-eligible individuals are also eligible for another veterans educational assistance program such as the Montgomery GI Bill-Active Duty (MGIB-AD; 38 U.S.C., Chapter 30), the Montgomery GI Bill-Selected Reserve (MGIB-SR; 10 U.S.C., Chapter 1606), Reserves Educational Assistance Program (REAP; 10 U.S.C., Chapter 1607), or Chapter 107 of Title 10 U.S.C. (professional military education). Individuals with a single qualifying active duty service period must make an *irrevocable* election to give up benefits under one other program to receive benefits under the Post-9/11 GI Bill. The individuals must be otherwise eligible for the Post-9/11 GI Bill.

Entitlement and Delimiting Date

The Post-9/11 GI Bill provides eligible persons an *entitlement* to educational assistance. This entitlement is measured in time—months and days. The entitlement period is 36 months (or its equivalent in part-time educational assistance). Generally, receipt of educational assistance payments for one day of full-time pursuit reduces the entitlement period by one day or a proportional percentage of a day for less-than-full-time pursuit. However, certain educational assistance payments reduce the entitlement period depending on the amount of the payment, as highlighted in the section on benefit payments.

In some instances, the entitlement period may be extended. The entitlement period is not reduced for individuals who must discontinue a course(s) and fail to receive credit or training time as a result of certain service obligations. For Reservists, a call to active duty under Section 688, 12301(a), 12301(d), 12301(g), 12302, or 12304 of Title 10 U.S.C. qualifies. For active duty servicemembers, assignment to a new duty location or an increased amount of work qualifies. In general, once the entitlement period is exhausted, eligible persons may continue receiving educational assistance through the end of the academic term if more than halfway through, or a 12-week period if not on an academic term schedule.

If individuals make an irrevocable election for the Post-9/11 GI Bill after using some entitlement under the MGIB-AD, MGIB-SR, or REAP, the Post-9/11 GI Bill entitlement is equal to the remaining months of entitlement under the other program. If individuals make an irrevocable election for the Post-9/11 GI Bill after exhausting their entitlement under the MGIB-AD, MGIB-SR, or REAP, the Post-9/11 GI Bill entitlement may be equal to 12 months.

---

[13] The Improvements Act required that, effective January 4, 2011, discharge or release as a result of a medical condition, hardship, or physical or mental condition qualify for Post-9/11 GI Bill benefits only if the active duty was characterized as honorable service.

By law, no educational benefits under the Post-9/11 GI Bill can be paid after the delimiting date—15 years or more after discharge or release from active duty.[14]

Eligible Programs of Education

Like most veterans educational assistance benefits, Post-9/11 GI Bill benefits can be used to support students pursuing approved programs of education at a variety of training establishments and educational institutions, including institutions of higher learning (IHLs).[15] The Improvements Act expanded the eligible programs of education beyond courses offered by an IHL, effective October 1, 2011, to include the following:

- courses at an *educational institution* (see below for the definition) that lead to a predetermined educational, vocational, or professional objective or objectives if related to the same career (this includes traditional undergraduate and graduate programs);

- courses required by the Administrator of the Small Business Administration (SBA) as a condition for obtaining financial assistance under the provisions of Section 7(i)(1) of the Small Business Act (15 U.S.C. 636(i)(1));

- licensing or certification tests for a predetermined vocation or profession, provided such tests and the licensing or credentialing organizations or entities that offer such tests are approved;

- courses offered by a qualified provider of entrepreneurship courses;

- national tests for admission to IHLs or graduate schools (such as the Scholastic Aptitude Test (SAT));

- national tests providing an opportunity for course credit at IHLs (such as the Advanced Placement (AP) exam);

- a preparatory course for a test that is required or used for admission to an institution of higher education or a graduate school;

---

[14] The 15-year limitation does not include periods when individuals were ineligible for the program but their discharge status was later amended to make them eligible for the program, and periods when individuals were detained by a foreign government or power and any related recovery period in a hospital. Individuals incapable of beginning education as a result of a physical or mental disability can be granted an extension for the period of incapacity.

[15] An institution of higher learning (IHL) is an institution offering postsecondary level academic instruction that leads to an associate's or higher degree if the school is empowered by the appropriate state education authority under state law to grant an associate's or higher degree, or in the absence of a state education authority, if the school is accredited for degree programs by a recognized accrediting agency. Institutions of higher learning are also hospitals offering educational programs at the postsecondary level and foreign educational institutions that offer courses leading to a standard college degree, or the equivalent, and that are recognized as such by the secretary of education (or a comparable official) of the country or other jurisdiction in which the institution is located. A standard college degree is an associate's or higher degree awarded by (1) an IHL that is accredited as a collegiate institution by a recognized regional or national accrediting agency; (2) an IHL that is a "candidate" for accreditation as that term is used by the regional or national accrediting agencies; or (3) an IHL upon completion of a course that is accredited by an agency recognized to accredit specialized degree-level programs.

- full-time programs of apprentice or other on-the-job training at a *training establishment* (see below for the definition), for individuals not on active duty;

- cooperative programs[16] for individuals not on active duty;

- refresher, remedial, or deficiency courses;[17]

- preparatory or special education or training courses necessary to enable the individual to pursue another approved program of education; and

- a course for which the individual is receiving Tuition Assistance from DOD (see the section entitled "Tuition Assistance "Top-Up" Program").[18]

The eligible programs of education must be approved by a state approving agency (SAA) or the VA, or must be deemed approved by statutory provisions. SAAs are federally authorized state entities that approve programs of education for the GI Bills. The VA provides some cost reimbursement of salaries and travel for the SAAs.

Educational institutions are defined as

- public or private elementary or secondary schools;

- vocational, correspondence, business, normal, or professional schools;

- colleges or universities;

- scientific or technical institutions;

- other institutions offering education for adults;

- state-approved alternative teacher certification program providers;

- private entities that offer courses toward the attainment of a license or certificate generally recognized as necessary for a profession or vocation in a high technology occupation; and

- qualified providers of entrepreneurship courses.

A **training establishment** is defined as

- an establishment providing apprentice or other on-the-job training;

- an establishment providing self-employment on-the-job training consisting of full-time training for a period of less than six months that is needed or accepted for purposes of obtaining licensure to engage in a self-employment occupation or

---

[16] A cooperative program is a full-time program of education, which consists of institutional courses and alternate phases of training in a business or industrial establishment with the training in a business or industrial establishment being strictly supplemental.

[17] A refresher course is a course at the elementary or secondary level that reviews or updates material previously covered in a course that has been satisfactorily completed, or a course which permits an individual to update knowledge and skills or be instructed in the technological advances which have occurred in the individual's field of employment during and since the period of the individual's active military service. A remedial course is a course designed to overcome a deficiency at the elementary or secondary level in a particular area of study, or a handicap, such as in speech. A deficiency course is any secondary level course or subject not previously completed satisfactorily, which is specifically required for pursuit of a postsecondary program of education.

[18] All programs of education must be approved by the VA and other relevant approving agencies.

required for ownership and operation of a franchise that is the objective of the training;

- a state board of vocational education;

- a federal or state apprenticeship registration agency;

- the sponsor of a program of apprenticeship; and

- an agency of the federal government authorized to supervise such training.

Benefit Payments

Under the Post-9/11 GI Bill, several types of benefit payments are available, including payments for tuition and fees, Yellow Ribbon payments,[19] housing allowance, books and supplies stipend, tutorial assistance, test fees, and relocation and travel assistance. The following describes the various payments and the criteria for determining the amount of each payment for which participants may be eligible.

Tuition and Fees, Housing, and Books and Supplies

The maximum payment levels for tuition and fees, housing, and books and supplies are summarized in **Table 1** by program of education. Many individuals will receive payments that are lower than these maximum payments as a result of the length of their qualifying active duty service (see **Table 2**), their enrollment rate or rate of pursuit, actual charges, active duty status, being enrolled exclusively through distance learning, and receipt of DOD Tuition Assistance (TA). Through TA, military service branches pay a certain amount of tuition and expenses for education and training to servicemembers on active duty and members of the Selected Reserve.[20] The Selected Reserve contains those military units and individuals that generally perform one weekend of training each month and two weeks of training each year for which they receive pay and benefits.

---

[19] Yellow Ribbon payments (see section entitled Yellow Ribbon G.I. Education Enhancement Program Payments) cover a portion of the tuition and fees that exceed the Post-9/11 GI Bill payments for tuition and fees.

[20] Title 10 U.S.C., Sections 2005 and 2007.

Table 1. Maximum Payments for Tuition and Fees, Housing, and Books and Supplies: Academic Year 2013-2014

Type of Education/Training	Tuition and Fees	Monthly Housing Allowance	Books and Supplies Stipend
More than half-time enrollment			
Non-active duty individuals in programs of education leading to a degree	At a public IHL,[a] "actual net cost for in-state tuition and fees" less certain student aid[b] At a private or foreign IHL,[a] up to $19,198.31;[c] or for certain prior enrollees through July 31, 2014, the greater of $17,500 or the benefit as calculated in 2010-2011[d]	E-5 with dependents BAH[e] in the military housing area in which the IHL is located	$1,000 per year
Active duty individuals in programs of education leading to a degree	At a public IHL,[a] "actual net cost for in-state tuition and fees" less certain student aid[b] At a private or foreign IHL,[a] $19,198.31[c]	None	$1,000 per year
Apprenticeship or on-the-job training	None	E-5 with dependents BAH[e] where the employer is located	$83 per month
Flight training	$10,970.46[c]	None	None
Correspondence training	$9,324.89[c]	None	None
Individuals in programs of education not leading to a degree	$19,198.31[c]	E-5 with dependents BAH[e] where the educational institution is located	$83 per month
Half-time or less enrollment			
Individuals enrolled half-time or less	At a public IHL,[a] "actual net cost for in-state tuition and fees" less certain student aid[b] At a private or foreign IHL,[a] $19,198.31[c]	None	$1,000 per year

Source: Table prepared by CRS based on Title 38 U.S.C., Chapter 33 and the Restoring GI Bill Fairness Act (P.L. 112-26).

Notes: Payments for many individuals will be lower than the maximum payments shown above based on the individual's length of qualifying active duty service, enrollment rate or rate of pursuit, active duty status, actual charges, being enrolled exclusively through distance learning, and receipt of U.S. Department of Defense (DOD) Tuition Assistance (TA). Under TA, military service branches may pay a certain amount of tuition and expenses for the education and training of active duty personnel and members of the Selected Reserve.

a. IHL is an institution of higher learning.

b. The forms of student aid that may be used to offset the "actual net cost for in-state tuition and fees" are certain waivers, reductions, scholarships, and assistance. The applicable scholarships and sources of assistance used to offset the actual tuition and fees are those provided directly to the IHL for the sole purpose of defraying tuition and fees. Loans and Pell Grants are specifically excluded from being used to offset the tuition and fees. Pell Grants are authorized by Section 401(b) of the Higher Education Act of 1965, as amended. For more information on Pell Grants, see CRS Report R42446, *Federal Pell Grant Program of the Higher Education Act: How the Program Works, Recent Legislative Changes, and Current Issues*, by Shannon M. Mahan.

c. The maximum established for the academic year beginning August 1, 2011, increases annually thereafter according to the average increase in undergraduate tuition in the United States as determined by the U.S. Department of Education (ED).

d. The Restoring GI Bill Fairness Act (P.L. 112-26) allows certain individuals through July 31, 2014, to receive a tuition and fees benefit equal to the greater of $17,500, reduced according to the length of time served on active duty, or the amount the individuals would have been entitled to in academic year (AY) 2010-2011 before the Improvements Act became effective. To be eligible, individuals must have been enrolled in the same private or foreign IHL since January 4, 2011, in a state in which the Post-9/11 GI Bill maximum in-state tuition per credit hour exceeded $700 in AY2010-2011 and the combined amount of tuition and fees for full-time attendance in the program of education in AY2010-2011 exceeded $17,500.

e. The E-5 with dependents BAH is the monthly basic allowance for housing for a member of the Armed Forces with dependents in pay grade E-5.

Table 2. Percentage of Maximum Post-9/11 GI Bill Benefits Based on Aggregate Length of Active Duty Service

Aggregate Time Served on Active Duty Since 9/11/2001	Percentage of Maximum Benefit Payable
At least 36 months	100
At least 30 continuous days on active duty and discharged due to service-connected disability	100
At least 30 months, but less than 36 months	90
At least 24 months, but less than 30 months	80
At least 18 months, but less than 24 months	70
At least 12 months, but less than 18 months	60
At least 6 months, but less than 12 months	50
At least 90 days, but less than 6 months	40

Source: Prepared by CRS based on Title 38 U.S.C. §3313 and data available from the U.S. Department of Veterans Affairs.

Non-active Duty Individuals Enrolled More than Half-Time in Programs of Education Leading to a Degree

Eligible individuals who are not on active duty, are pursuing a program of education in residence or online leading to a degree at an IHL, and are enrolled more than half-time may receive the following payments for tuition and fees, housing, and books and supplies:

*   *Tuition and fees.* Individuals attending public IHLs in programs of education leading to a degree are eligible to receive payments equal to the "actual net cost for in-state tuition and fees" for the program of education, reduced according to the length of time served on active duty (**Table 2**) and less certain waivers, reductions, scholarships, and assistance.[21] For academic year (AY) 2013-2014 with one exception (see box below), individuals attending private or foreign IHLs in programs of education leading to a degree are eligible to receive the lesser of $19,198.31,[22] reduced according to the length of time served on active duty

---

[21] The "actual net cost for tuition and fees" is not defined.

[22] The maximum of $17,500 for the academic year beginning August 1, 2011, increases annually thereafter according (continued...)

(**Table 2**), or the "actual net cost for tuition and fees" for the program of education less certain waivers, reductions, scholarships, and assistance and reduced according to the length of time served on active duty (**Table 2**). The applicable scholarships and sources of assistance used to offset the "actual net cost for tuition and fees" are those provided directly to the IHL for the sole purpose of defraying tuition and fees. The applicable scholarships and assistance specifically exclude loans and Pell Grants.[23] The tuition and fees benefit is paid directly to the IHL for each academic term.

Tuition and Fees Payments for Selected Individuals Attending Private IHLs

Exception to the tuition and fees benefit amount is made for individuals who have been enrolled in the same private IHL since January 4, 2011, in a state in which the Post-9/11 GI Bill maximum in-state tuition per credit hour exceeded $700 in AY2010-2011 and the combined amount of tuition and fees for full-time attendance in the program of education in academic year (AY) 2010-2011 exceeded $17,500.[24] The affected states are Arizona, Michigan, New Hampshire, New York, Pennsylvania, South Carolina, and Texas. Through July 31, 2014, the excepted individuals are eligible for the greater of $17,500, reduced according to the length of time served on active duty (**Table 2**), or the amount the individuals would have been entitled to in AY2010-2011 before the Improvements Act became effective.[25]

In AY2010-2011, eligible individuals who were not on active duty, were pursuing a program of education at an IHL, and were enrolled more than half-time received the following payments for tuition and fees:

- *Tuition.* A per credit hour enrolled tuition payment was made directly to the IHL for each academic term in an amount equal to that charged the veteran or a percentage of the maximum amount of undergraduate in-state tuition charged for the same number of credit hours at the most expensive public institution in the state in which the individual was enrolled, whichever was less. The percentage of the maximum undergraduate tuition was determined by the length of time served on active duty (**Table 2**). There was great variation among the states, ranging from a low of $90 per credit hour in Puerto Rico to a high of $1,549 in Texas for AY2010-2011.[26]

   For example, a Post-9/11 GI Bill eligible veteran with 28 months of qualifying active duty service may have chosen to enroll as a full-time undergraduate at XYZ College in Michigan in AY2010-2011. XYZ College defines full-time attendance as 24 credit hours. The veteran would have been eligible to receive 80% of the maximum benefit because the veteran served 28 months on active duty. The maximum tuition benefit in Michigan was $1,001 per credit hour for AY2010-2011. In AY2010-2011, XYZ College charged approximately $35,508 for full-time (24 credit hours) undergraduate tuition.[27] The veteran would have received the lesser of $19,219 (80% × $1,001 per credit hour × 24 credit hours) or the actual tuition charged ($35,508) in Post-9/11 GI Bill tuition benefits. The VA would have sent a total of $19,219 to XYZ College over the academic year on behalf of the veteran for tuition. The veteran would have had an out of pocket tuition cost of $16,289 ($35,508 - $19,219). The VA would not have remitted more tuition than the veteran was charged by the institution.

(...continued)

to the average increase in undergraduate tuition in the United States as determined by the U.S. Department of Education (ED).

[23] Pell Grants are authorized by Section 401(b) of the Higher Education Act of 1965, as amended. For more information on Pell Grants, see CRS Report R42446, *Federal Pell Grant Program of the Higher Education Act: How the Program Works, Recent Legislative Changes, and Current Issues*, by Shannon M. Mahan.

[24] Restoring GI Bill Fairness Act of 2011 (P.L. 112-26).

[25] The benefit amount for excepted individuals does not increase annually based on an inflation index.

[26] Although California's public colleges and universities only charge fees and do not charge resident undergraduate tuition, the VA and the California state approving agency reached an agreement to break up the fees into a tuition charge and fees charge for the purposes of the Post-9/11 GI Bill. U.S. Department of Veterans Affairs, 2010-11 Maximum In-State Tuition and Fees, available at http://www.gibill.va.gov/GI_Bill_Info/CH33/Tuition_and_fees.htm, last updated August 30, 2010.

[27] Tuition was reported to ED in the Integrated Postsecondary Education Data System (IPEDS).

- *Fees*. A fees payment was made directly to the IHL for each academic term in an amount equal to that charged to the veteran or a percentage of the maximum amount of undergraduate fees charged at the most expensive public institution in the state in which the individual was enrolled, whichever was less. The percentage of the maximum undergraduate fees was determined by the length of time served on active duty (**Table 2**). There was great variation among the states, ranging from a low of $249 in Guam to a high of $85,255 in Utah for each academic term in AY2010-2011.[28]

Through July 31, 2014, eligible individuals in Arizona, Michigan, New Hampshire, New York, Pennsylvania, South Carolina, and Texas will be eligible for the greater of $17,500, reduced according to the length of time served on active duty (**Table 2**), or the following:

State	Maximum Tuition Charge per Credit Hour ($)	Maximum Total Fees per Term ($)
Arizona	725.00	15,000.00
Michigan	1,001.00	19,374.50
New Hampshire	1,003.75	5,197.00
New York	1,010.00	12,293.00
Pennsylvania	934.00	6,110.00
South Carolina	829.00	2,798.00
Texas	1,549.00	12,130.00

- *Housing Allowance*. The housing allowance is based on the DOD-determined monthly basic allowance for housing (BAH) for a member of the Armed Forces with dependents in pay grade E-5 (hereinafter referred to as the *E-5 with dependents BAH*).[29] For individuals not enrolled exclusively through distance learning,[30] the monthly housing allowance equals the E-5 with dependents BAH in the military housing area in which the IHL is located, reduced according to the length of time served on active duty (**Table 2**) and the individual's enrollment rate (rounded to the nearest multiple of 10). For example, an individual enrolled in 10 credit hours, assuming 12 credit hours as full-time, receives 80% of the E-5 with dependents BAH where the IHL is located, reduced according to the length of time served on active duty (**Table 2**). The E-5 with dependents BAH for attendance at foreign institutions equals the national average of the E-5 with dependents BAH. For individuals enrolled exclusively through distance learning,

---

[28] High fees are often related to flight training and schools of pharmacy. U.S. Department of Veterans Affairs, 2010-11 Maximum In-State Tuition and Fees, available at http://www.gibill.va.gov/GI_Bill_Info/CH33/Tuition_and_fees.htm, last updated August 30, 2010.

[29] BAH is a DOD benefit to uniformed servicemembers to provide housing compensation when government quarters are not provided. The amount is based on a survey of actual median current market rent, average utilities (including electricity, heat, and water/sewer), and average renter's insurance in local civilian housing markets and is payable based on geographic duty location, pay grade, and dependency status.

[30] Distance education is defined in 20 U.S.C. §1003(6) as education to deliver instruction to students who are separated from the instructor and to support regular and substantive interaction between the students and the instructor, synchronously or asynchronously, that uses one or more of the following technologies: the Internet; one- and two-way transmissions through open broadcast, closed circuit, cable, microwave, broadband lines, fiber optics, satellite, or wireless communications devices; audio conferencing; or video cassettes, DVDs, and CD-ROMs, if the cassettes, DVDs, or CD-ROMs are used in a course in conjunction with the Internet, one- and two-way transmissions, or audio conferencing.

the monthly housing allowance is 50% of the national average of the E-5 with dependents BAH, reduced according to the length of time served on active duty (**Table 2**) and the individual's enrollment rate.[31] The housing allowance is paid directly to eligible individuals monthly. There is great variation among the localities in the United States, ranging from a low of $840 in the Klamath Falls, OR, area to a high of $3,744 in the New York City area in calendar year 2014.[32]

- *Books and Supplies Stipend.* Individuals also receive a maximum stipend of $1,000 per year for books and required educational expenses. The stipend is paid monthly directly to eligible individuals based on the number of credit hours, or their equivalent, in which individuals are enrolled each term. Each credit hour, or its equivalent, is worth $41.67, reduced according to the length of time served on active duty (**Table 2**).[33] This stipend does not reduce the entitlement period and does not reduce other benefit payments.

Active Duty Individuals Enrolled More than Half-Time in Programs of Education Leading to a Degree

Individuals serving on active duty while enrolled more than half-time in programs of education leading to a degree may receive the following payments for tuition and fees, housing, and books and supplies:

- *Tuition and fees.* The tuition and fees benefit is paid directly to the IHL on behalf of eligible individuals for each academic term. The benefit amount is the lesser of

  - at a public IHL, the "actual net cost for in-state tuition and fees" for the program of education, reduced according to the length of time served on active duty (**Table 2**) and less certain waivers, reductions, scholarships, and assistance;

  - at a private or foreign IHL for AY2013-2014, the lesser of $19,198.31,[34] reduced according to the length of time served on active duty (**Table 2**), or the "actual net cost for tuition and fees" for the program of education, reduced according to the length of time served on active duty (**Table 2**) and less certain waivers, reductions, scholarships, and assistance; or

  - the amount allowable under the Tuition Assistance "Top-Up" Program (see the subsequent section entitled Tuition Assistance "Top-Up" Program).[35]

---

[31] Individuals in a program offered exclusively through distance learning were not eligible for a Post-9/11 GI Bill housing allowance until September 30, 2011, as a result of the Improvements Act.

[32] U.S. Department of Defense, *BAH Rates for All Locations*, available at http://www.defensetravel.dod mil/site/bah.cfm as of July 10, 2014.

[33] The VA has determined in 38 CFR 21.9640 that a lump sum books and supplies stipend for each academic term equals $41.67 multiplied by the number of credit hours enrolled and multiplied by the ratio of the number of credit hours enrolled to the number of credit hours required for full-time pursuit.

[34] The maximum of $17,500 for the academic year beginning August 1, 2011, increases annually thereafter according to the average increase in undergraduate tuition in the United States as determined by ED.

[35] Prior to an Improvements Act amendment, which went into effect March 5, 2011, individuals on active duty received (payable to the IHL) the amount of tuition and fees charged by the IHL, as long as the amount did not duplicate any amounts received through a DOD Tuition Assistance Program. This amount could exceed amounts charged by the most expensive public institution in the state. The entitlement period was reduced one month for each month enrolled.

- *Housing Allowance*. Individuals who are in programs of education leading to a degree and serving on active duty are ineligible to receive a Post-9/11 GI Bill housing allowance.

- *Books and Supplies Stipend*. Individuals enrolled more than half-time in programs of education leading to a degree while on active duty receive for each academic term a lump sum stipend for books and supplies in the amount of $1,000, reduced according to the length of time served on active duty (**Table 2**) and according to the proportion of a complete academic year that such academic term constitutes.[36]

Individuals Pursuing Apprenticeship or On-the-Job Training More than Half-Time

Individuals pursuing apprenticeship or on-the-job training more than half-time may receive the following payments for tuition and fees, housing, and books and supplies:[37]

- *Tuition and fees*. Individuals pursuing apprenticeship or on-the-job training more than half-time are ineligible to receive a tuition and fees benefit.

- *Housing Allowance*. Individuals pursuing apprenticeship or on-the-job training more than half-time receive a monthly housing allowance equal to 100%, 80%, 60%, 40%, and 20% of the E-5 with dependents BAH where the employer is located for the first six months, second six months, third six months, fourth six months, and thereafter, respectively. The housing allowance is further reduced depending on the length of time served on qualifying active duty (**Table 2**) and by the proportion of working/training hours completed each month that is below 120.

- *Books and Supplies Stipend*. Individuals pursuing apprenticeship or on-the-job training more than half-time receive a books and supplies stipend each academic term in the amount of $83 per month, reduced according to the length of time served on active duty (**Table 2**).

Flight Trainees Enrolled More than Half-Time

Individuals enrolled more than half-time in programs of education consisting of flight training may receive the following payments for tuition and fees, housing, and books and supplies:[38]

- *Tuition and fees*. For AY2012-2013, individuals enrolled more than half-time in flight training receive a tuition and fees benefit equal to the lesser of

---

[36] Prior to an Improvements Act amendment, which went into effect October 1, 2011, individuals on active duty did not receive a books and supplies stipend.

[37] The Improvements Act expanded the eligible programs of education to include apprenticeship and on-the-job training effective October 1, 2011.

[38] The Improvements Act expanded the eligible programs of education to include flight training from non-IHLs effective October 1, 2011. Statute establishes the payment amounts for "flight training (regardless of the institution providing such program of education)," but the VA has indicated that it is not implementing the described payment amounts for degree programs that consist of flight training at IHLs (http://gibill.va.gov/resources/education_resources/programs/flight_training html).

$10,970.46,[39] reduced according to the length of time served on qualifying active duty (see **Table 2**), or the "actual net cost for in-state tuition and fees" for the program of education, less certain waivers, reductions, scholarships, and assistance. The tuition and fees benefit is paid to the educational institution after individuals complete the training.

- *Housing Allowance*. Individuals pursuing flight training are ineligible to receive a housing allowance.

- *Books and Supplies Stipend*. Individuals pursuing flight training are ineligible to receive a books and supplies stipend.

Correspondence Trainees Enrolled More than Half-Time

Correspondence training differs from distance learning or online education in that individuals in correspondence training usually receive lessons in the mail and have a certain amount of time to complete and return them for a grade. Individuals enrolled more than half-time exclusively in correspondence training programs, regardless of the type of institution, may receive the following payments for tuition and fees, housing, and books and supplies:[40]

- *Tuition and fees*. For AY2012-2013, individuals enrolled exclusively in correspondence training more than half-time receive a tuition and fees benefit equal to the lesser of $9,324.89,[41] reduced according to the length of time served on qualifying active duty (see **Table 2**), or the "actual net cost for tuition and fees" for the program of education less certain waivers, reductions, scholarships, and assistance. The tuition and fees benefit is paid to the educational institution after the individuals complete the training.

- *Housing Allowance*. Individuals pursuing correspondence training exclusively are ineligible to receive a housing allowance.

- *Books and Supplies Stipend*. Individuals pursuing correspondence training exclusively are ineligible to receive a books and supplies stipend.

Individuals Enrolled More than Half-Time in Programs of Education Not Leading to a Degree

Active duty and non-active duty individuals who are enrolled more than half-time at a non-college degree granting institution, referred to by statute as a certificate or non-college degree program at an institution or establishment other than an IHL that is not on-the-job, apprenticeship, flight, or correspondence training, may receive the following payments for tuition and fees, housing, and books and supplies:[42]

---

[39] The maximum of $10,000 for the academic year beginning August 1, 2011, increases annually thereafter according to the average increase in undergraduate tuition in the United States as determined by ED.

[40] The Improvements Act expanded the eligible programs of education to include correspondence training effective October 1, 2011.

[41] The maximum of $8,500 for the academic year beginning August 1, 2011, increases annually thereafter according to the average increase in undergraduate tuition in the United States as determined by ED.

[42] The Improvements Act expanded the eligible programs of education to include certificate and non-college degree programs at non-IHLs, effective October 1, 2011.

- *Tuition and fees.* Individuals enrolled more than half-time in programs of education not leading to a degree receive a tuition and fees benefit equal to the lesser of $19,198.31,[43] reduced according to the length of time served on qualifying active duty (see **Table 2**), or the "actual net cost for in-state tuition and fees" less certain waivers, reductions, scholarships, and assistance. The tuition and fees benefit is paid to the educational institution each academic term.

- *Housing Allowance.* For individuals pursuing a program of education in-residence, the monthly housing allowance is equal to the E-5 with dependents BAH where the educational institution is located, reduced according to the length of time served on qualifying active duty (see **Table 2**) and in proportion to the enrollment rate. Individuals pursuing a program of education through distance learning receive 50% of the amount received by individuals pursuing a program of education in-residence.

- *Books and Supplies Stipend.* Individuals enrolled more than half-time in programs of education not leading to a degree receive a books and supplies stipend in the amount of $83 per month paid to the individuals for each academic term, reduced according to the length of time served on qualifying active duty (see **Table 2**).

Individuals Enrolled Half-Time or Less

Individuals enrolled half-time or less in any program of education and regardless of the active duty status may receive the following payments for tuition and fees, housing, and books and supplies:

- *Tuition and fees.* Individuals enrolled half-time or less are eligible for a tuition and fees benefit of the "actual net cost for in-state tuition and fees" assessed by the IHL less certain waivers, reductions, scholarships, and assistance, but not more than the amount for which the individuals would have been eligible if enrolled more than half-time in a program of education leading to a degree at an IHL.[44]

- *Housing Allowance.* Individuals enrolled half-time or less are ineligible to receive a housing allowance.

- *Books and Supplies Stipend.* Individuals enrolled half-time or less may receive a books and supplies stipend that is a percentage of the maximum stipend of $1,000 per year, reduced in proportion to their enrollment rate. The percentage of the stipend is determined by the length of time served on active duty (**Table 2**).

---

[43] The maximum of $17,500 for the academic year beginning August 1, 2011, increases annually thereafter according to the average increase in undergraduate tuition in the United States as determined by the ED.

[44] Prior to an Improvements Act amendment, which went into effect August 1, 2011, individuals enrolled half-time or less received (payable to the IHL) the amount charged by the IHL, but not more than the amount the individual would have been eligible to receive if enrolled full-time.

Yellow Ribbon GI Education Enhancement Program Payments

In cases in which an IHL's tuition and fees are not fully covered by the tuition and fees payment benefits, the IHL may voluntarily enter into a Yellow Ribbon Program agreement with the VA to match an equal percentage of some portion of the remaining tuition and fees. Yellow Ribbon Program agreements benefit participants enrolled in private IHLs and enrolled as out-of-state students at public IHLs.

The Yellow Ribbon Program covers a portion of the tuition and fees that exceed the base Post-9/11 GI Bill tuition and fees benefit. The Yellow Ribbon Program payment is paid equally by the IHL and the VA. The program allows IHLs to enter into agreements with the VA to match a certain amount of the tuition and fees not already covered by the basic Post-9/11 GI Bill. Each IHL must establish the number of eligible individuals it is willing to support and how much it is willing to contribute for each individual. VA regulations allow IHLs to specify their support by each sub-element: college or professional school; and by student status: undergraduate, graduate, or doctoral. Several IHLs have variously agreed to support between one and an unlimited number of eligible students for an amount from $50 per semester to the maximum amount needed by the student (see box below for an example of how the Yellow Ribbon program works).

The program is only available to individuals at the 100% benefit level and the dependents to whom they have transferred benefits. As long as the IHL remains in the Yellow Ribbon Program, individuals admitted under the program who maintain satisfactory progress will continue to be supported under the program.

Example of Yellow Ribbon Program Payments

Participant: A Post-9/11 GI Bill eligible veteran with 36 months of qualifying active duty service may choose to enroll as a full-time law student at the private ABC University in Washington.

University charges: ABC University defines full-time attendance as 30 credit hours and charges $35,987.00 ($1,177.00 per credit hour for tuition * 30 credits for full-time attendance + $677.00 per year in fees) in AY2012-2013.

Base Post-9/11 GI Bill tuition and fees benefit: For individuals at the 100% benefit level attending private IHLs in programs of education leading to a degree, the tuition and fees benefit is the lesser of $18,077.50 or the "actual net cost for tuition and fees" for the program of education less certain waivers, reductions, scholarships, and assistance. Assuming the Post-9/11 GI Bill eligible veteran does not receive waivers, reductions, scholarships, or assistance, the base Post-9/11 GI Bill tuition and fees benefit is $18,077.50 (the lesser of $18,077.50 and $35,987.00).

Unpaid balance: $17,909.50 ($35,987.00 - $18,077.50)

ABC Yellow Ribbon Program Agreement: Maximum of $8,905.00 per law student per year for seven law students.

Yellow Ribbon Program Payments: If the veteran in this example is one of the seven students eligible for the Yellow Ribbon program at ABC's law school, the VA will match the university's payment up to $8,905 per year for a total maximum benefit of $17,810.00 ($8,905.00 * 2). Since the maximum benefit is less than the unpaid balance, the VA will make a Yellow Ribbon payment of $8,905.00 and ABC will make a Yellow Ribbon payment of $8,905.00.

Out-of-pocket cost: $99.50 ($17,909.50 - $17,810.00)

Total Post-9/11 GI Bill benefits: The VA will have paid $26,982.50 ($18,077.50 in basic tuition and fees benefit + $8,905.00 in Yellow Ribbon payments) on behalf of the veteran. Post-9/11 GI Bill benefits will provide the veteran a total of $35,887.50 ($26,982.50 from the VA + $8,905.00 from the university) for tuition and fees.

Tutorial Assistance

Individuals are entitled to payment, not to exceed $100 monthly and up to a maximum of $1,200 over the course of the entitlement period, for tutorial assistance provided the IHL certifies that the individuals need tutoring to pass a course(s) required for the approved program of education. The maximum tutorial assistance is not reduced depending on the length of qualifying active duty service. Tutorial assistance does not reduce the entitlement period and does not reduce other benefit payments.

Licensing and Certification Test Fees

A fee of up to $2,000 may be reimbursed for each approved licensing or certification test as long as the payment does not exceed the individual's remaining Post-9/11 GI Bill entitlement.[45] The benefit is available regardless of whether individuals pass the test. For AY2013-2014, the entitlement charge is one month (rounded to the nearest whole non-zero month) for each payment that equals $1,601.69.[46] Therefore, each test reduces an individual's entitlement by a minimum of one month. Neither the benefit nor the entitlement charge will depend on the length of qualifying active duty service.

National Tests

Individuals may receive reimbursement for a national test for admission to an IHL and a national test providing an opportunity for course credit at an IHL.[47] The maximum benefit for a test will be the individual's remaining Post-9/11 GI Bill entitlement. For AY2013-2013, the entitlement charge is one month (rounded to the nearest whole non-zero month) for each payment that equals $1,601.69.[48] Therefore, each test reduces an individual's entitlement by a minimum of one month.

Relocation and Travel Assistance

Individuals who reside in rural counties and who either relocate a distance of at least 500 miles to pursue a program of education or must travel by air to attend an IHL are entitled to a single payment of up to $500. The relocation assistance does not reduce the entitlement period, does not reduce other benefit payments, and is not reduced depending on the length of qualifying active duty service.

---

[45] Prior to an Improvements Act amendment, which went into effect August 1, 2011, individuals were eligible for a fee of up to $2,000 for *one* approved licensing or certification test. The maximum fee was not reduced depending on the length of active duty service. The fee did not reduce the entitlement period and did not reduce other benefit payments under the Post-9/11 GI Bill.

[46] The equivalent entitlement charge of $1,460 for the academic year beginning August 1, 2011, increases annually thereafter according to the average increase in undergraduate tuition in the United States as determined by ED.

[47] The Improvements Act allowed reimbursement for national tests effective August 1, 2011.

[48] The equivalent entitlement charge of $1,460 for the academic year beginning August 1, 2011, increases annually thereafter according to the average increase in undergraduate tuition in the United States as determined by ED.

Advance Payments

An advance payment is the first partial and first full month of the housing allowance and is available to individuals who are planning to enroll more than half-time and who have not received educational assistance benefits in 30 days or more. Advance payments are sent to the educational institution for disbursal to the student within 30 days of the start of the academic term. Although regulations clarify the eligibility requirements for advance payments of the monthly housing allowance, VA guidance and policy documents indicate that advance payments are not available under the Post-9/11 GI Bill.[49]

Supplemental Assistance

Military service branches may provide various incentives to recruit and retain high quality individuals in the Armed Forces. Eligible recruits and servicemembers may be given a choice of one of several incentives such as cash bonuses. *Supplemental assistance for additional years of service* and *supplemental assistance for critical skills (Kickers)* are incentives that are realized when the individuals use their GI Bill benefit. The expected benefit amount is deposited into the DOD Educational Benefits Trust Fund until the individuals take advantage of the benefit, at which time the benefit amount is transferred to the VA for payment.[50] The supplemental assistance, up to $950, is added to the individuals' monthly GI Bill payment, including the Post-9/11 GI Bill monthly housing allowance. As a result, individuals who enroll half-time or less or who are serving on active duty are not eligible because they are not eligible to receive a housing allowance.[51] The amount may be reduced depending on the individuals' time served on active duty and, for individuals who make an irrevocable election to receive Post-9/11 GI Bill benefits in lieu of benefits under the MGIB-AD or MGIB-SR, in proportion to the enrollment rate.[52]

Supplemental assistance for additional years of service may be offered to either individuals in the active component who agree to remain on active duty for at least five additional continuous years, or to individuals in the Selected Reserve who agree to serve at least two additional consecutive years on active duty and at least four additional consecutive years in the Selected Reserve.

Supplemental assistance for critical skills may be offered either to recruit into the regular Armed Forces enlistees with critical skills or to gain agreement from individuals with critical skills to serve in the Selected Reserve after separating honorably from the regular Armed Forces. A critical skill is a skill or specialty in which there is a critical shortage or for which it is difficult to recruit or, in the case of critical units, retain personnel.

---

[49] 38 C.F.R. §21.9680(b)(2); U.S. Department of Veterans Affairs, *School Certifying Official Handbook*, 3rd Edition, Revision 2: 09/30/13, p. 63; and U.S. Department of Education, "Am I eligible for an advance payment of my education benefits?," Frequently Asked Questions, October 4, 2011, https://gibill.custhelp.com/app/answers/list.

[50] Funding may also be paid from Department of Homeland Security (DHS) appropriations.

[51] Office of the Under Secretary of Defense, *Directive-Type Memorandum (DTM) 09-003: Post-9/11 GI Bill*, June 22, 2009, Incorporating Change 2, September 14, 2011.

[52] The Improvements Act reduced the supplemental assistance in proportion to the enrollment rate, effective August 1, 2011.

Tuition Assistance "Top-Up" Program

The Tuition Assistance "Top-Up" program was established under the Floyd D. Spence National Defense Authorization Act for Fiscal Year 2001 (P.L. 106-398) to promote retention. Under Tuition Assistance Top-Up, Post-9/11 GI Bill-eligible servicemembers receiving TA benefits on active duty may elect to receive Post-9/11 GI Bill benefits to pay tuition and fees charges above the amount paid by TA. Individuals may not receive more Post-9/11 GI Bill benefits than the individuals would have otherwise been eligible. The amount of Top-Up is not reduced by the length of time served on qualifying active duty. Entitlement is charged one month for each month enrolled full-time and proportionally reduced based on the enrollment rate.

Unused MGIB-AD Contributions

Individuals are generally required to make a $1,200 contribution to be eligible for MGIB-AD benefits. For individuals who make an irrevocable election to receive Post-9/11 GI Bill benefits in lieu of MGIB-AD benefits, their unused MGIB-AD contributions are refunded as an addition to the last Post-9/11 GI Bill monthly housing allowance once the entitlement period is exhausted. If individuals are not eligible for the monthly housing allowance or fail to exhaust the entitlement period, the unused MGIB-AD contributions are not refunded.

MGIB-AD Buy Up Program

Under the MGIB-AD $600 Buy-Up program, servicemembers may contribute up to $600 to the military service branch in multiples of $20 and receive for every $20 contributed up to an additional $5 every month (up to $5,400 total) during which the individuals receive MGIB-AD benefits. Individuals in the Post-9/11 GI Bill forfeit any contributions to the $600 MGIB-AD Buy Up program.

Marine Gunnery Sergeant John David Fry Scholarship Program

The Supplemental Appropriations Act of 2009 (P.L. 111-32) amended the Post-9/11 GI Bill to create the Marine Gunnery Sergeant John David Fry Scholarship. The scholarship program is available to the children of individuals who, on or after September 11, 2001, die in the line of duty while serving on active duty as a member of the Armed Forces. Children are unmarried or married persons and unmarried persons who became permanently incapable of self-support before the age of 18. Children include children born outside of marriage and acknowledged, legally adopted children, and stepchildren who are members of the households of eligible individuals. The Armed Forces include the Reserves and National Guard, but exclude the Public Health Service (PHS) and National Oceanic and Atmospheric Administration (NOAA). Scholarship recipients are eligible to receive all applicable Post-9/11 GI Bill benefits, except Yellow Ribbon payments, for 36 months at the maximum 100% rate. Children who are serving on active duty will receive benefits like other servicemembers on active duty.[53] No scholarship

---

[53] U.S. Department of Veterans Affairs, "Post-9/11 GI Bill: Marine Gunnery Sergeant John David Fry Scholarship," press release, http://www.gibill.va.gov/documents/Fry_Scholarship.pdf.

program benefits can be paid 15 years or more after the child's 18th birthday. Although the program took effect August 1, 2009, payments, including retroactive payments, were not made until August 1, 2010.

Transferability to Dependents

The DOD allows the transfer of benefits from individuals eligible for the Post-9/11 GI Bill to certain family members. In order to designate to whom the Post-9/11 GI Bill-eligible individuals want to transfer benefits, individuals must be currently members of the Armed Forces (active duty or Selected Reserve). In other words, individuals who have retired or been separated are no longer eligible to designate a transferee. As of August 1, 2011, and September 1, 2011, as authorized by the Improvements Act, active duty members of the Commissioned Corps of the PHS and NOAA, respectively, are eligible to transfer unused Post-9/11 GI Bill education benefits to their eligible dependents.

Three categories of individuals in the Armed Forces, including PHS and NOAA, may designate to whom they are transferring some or all of their benefits. The first category includes members of the Armed Forces who have completed at least six years of service (active duty or Selected Reserve) and agree to serve four additional years. The second category includes members of the Armed Forces who have completed at least 10 years of service and are precluded from serving an additional four years by either standard policy or statute but agree to serve the maximum amount of time allowable. The third category includes members of the Armed Forces who became retirement eligible between August 1, 2009, and July 31, 2012.[54]

Individuals eligible to transfer their benefits can transfer up to 36 months of benefits to their child, to their spouse, or to some combination of children and spouse. The family members must be enrolled in the DOD Defense Eligibility Enrollment Reporting System (DEERS) and be eligible for benefits at the time the transfer is designated. The eligible member of the Armed Forces can designate the family member, the number of months of the entitlement period, and the period during which it may be used. After retirement or separation from the Armed Forces, individuals can only modify the number of months of the transferred entitlement period or revoke the designation. After retirement or separation from the Armed Forces, individuals cannot designate new family members. As dependents use the transferred benefit, the remaining entitlement periods of both the dependents and members of the Armed Forces are reduced. The designees can use the benefit for the same purposes as the eligible individuals and for the completion of a high school diploma or its equivalent.

A spouse can begin using the benefit after the servicemember completes at least six years of service. Spouses who subsequently divorce Post-9/11 GI Bill-eligible individuals are still eligible to use the transferred benefits unless the eligible individuals revoke the transfer.[55] The spouses receive payments according to the current status of the eligible individuals. The spouses may use

---

[54] Servicemembers who became eligible for retirement on August 1, 2009, were not required to serve additional time. Servicemembers who became eligible for retirement after August 1, 2009, and before August 1, 2010, were required to serve one additional year of service. Servicemembers who became eligible for retirement on or after August 1, 2010, and before August 1, 2011, were required to serve two additional years of service. Servicemembers who became eligible for retirement on or after August 1, 2011, and before August 1, 2012, are required to serve three additional years of service.

[55] The transferred benefits cannot be considered marital property in divorce proceedings.

the benefits within 15 years of the eligible individual's discharge or release from active duty service.

Children have to achieve a high school diploma, achieve the equivalent of a high school diploma, or reach 18 years of age before using the benefit. In addition, the servicemember has to complete at least 10 years of service before a designated child can use the benefit. Children receive payments as if the eligible individuals were not on active duty. Children must use the benefit before reaching 26 years of age.[56]

Relationship to Other Veterans Educational Assistance Programs

Many servicemembers are eligible for more than one veterans educational assistance program. Individuals who served on active duty after June 30, 1985, may be eligible for the Montgomery GI Bill-Active Duty (MGIB-AD; 38 U.S.C., Chapter 30); and reservists who served on active duty after September 10, 2001, may be eligible for the Reserves Educational Assistance Program (REAP; 10 U.S.C., Chapter 1607). Individuals who are serving in the Selected Reserve may be eligible for the Montgomery GI Bill-Selected Reserve (MGIB-SR; 10 U.S.C., Chapter 1606). Individuals who have served in the Armed Forces and who are or were the dependents of servicemembers who were disabled, delayed,[57] or died as a result of military service may be eligible for the Survivors' and Dependents' Educational Assistance program (DEA; 38 U.S.C., Chapter 35).[58] Statutory provisions govern how and to what extent benefits from different programs may be used.

In most instances, individuals with a single qualifying active duty service period or event must elect the program to which such service is to be credited. For example, a reservist who served on active duty for 36 months starting in 2003 may be eligible for the Post-9/11 GI Bill, MGIB-AD, and REAP, however, the reservist must elect to give up eligibility to one program. Individuals who are eligible for both the Post-9/11 GI Bill Fry Scholarship and DEA benefits based on the death of the same parent must elect the program from which to receive benefits.[59] This decision is generally irrevocable.

With a few exceptions, veterans and servicemembers with more than one qualifying active duty service period or event can generally combine benefit programs administered by the VA to receive no more than 48 months of educational benefits.[60] Individuals eligible for the Post-9/11

---

[56] Effective August 1, 2011, the Improvements Act grants an extension of the entitlement period to children to whom Post-9/11 GI Bill benefits are transferred and who are incapable of pursuing their chosen program of education before age 26 as a result of being the primary caregiver, according to the family caregiver assistance program (38 U.S.C. §1720G(a)).

[57] A servicemember is delayed if the person is listed as missing in action, captured in the line of duty, or forcibly detained as a result of active duty service.

[58] For information on DEA, see CRS Report R40723, *Educational Assistance Programs Administered by the U.S. Department of Veterans Affairs*, by Cassandria Dortch (available upon request).

[59] An Improvements Act amendment established this requirement effective August 1, 2011.

[60] Aggregate educational assistance may not exceed 48 months under the following programs: Parts VII or VIII, Veterans Regulation numbered 1(a), as amended; Title II of the Veterans' Readjustment Assistance Act of 1952; the War Orphans' Educational Assistance Act of 1956; Chapters 30, 32, 33, 34, and 36 of Title 38 U.S.C. and the former (continued...)

GI Bill based on their service and eligible for transferred Post-9/11 GI Bill benefits are not subject to the 48-month limit.[61] Effective October 1, 2013, DEA-eligible individuals who are also eligible for another GI Bill program may combine benefit programs to receive up to 81 months of entitlement.[62] However, benefits under more than one program cannot be received concurrently.

Relationship to the Vocational Rehabilitation and Employment Program (VR&E)

Post-9/11 GI Bill-eligible individuals who receive benefits from the Vocational Rehabilitation and Employment Program (VR&E) program are eligible for an alternative subsistence allowance.[63] VR&E participants receive a subsistence allowance based on the number of dependents, type of education or training pursued, and rate of attendance. Effective October 1, 2013, the regular subsistence allowance for full-time training at an IHL is $868.96 monthly for individuals with two dependents. Individuals eligible for both VR&E and the Post-9/11 GI Bill may choose to receive the regular subsistence allowance or the E-5 with dependents BAH for the zip code in which the rehabilitation program is located.[64]

VR&E is an entitlement program that provides job training and related services to veterans with service-connected disabilities. To be entitled to VR&E services, a veteran must have received a discharge other than dishonorable and be found to have either (1) a 20% service-connected disability and an employment handicap, or (2) a 10% service-connected disability and a serious employment handicap.[65] After a veteran is found to be entitled to VR&E, a counselor helps the veteran identify a suitable employment goal and determine what services will be necessary to achieve that goal. The veteran is then assigned to one of five reemployment tracks, one of which may include postsecondary or vocational training.

The reemployment track that includes postsecondary or vocational training, referred to as the Employment through Long-Term Services track, provides participants up to 48 months (or the part-time equivalent) to achieve their objective within 12 years of discharge or release. The VA may extend the entitlement period if necessary to accomplish the rehabilitation program.

While pursuing their objective, the progress of individuals is tracked and reviewed by case managers to ensure the veterans have all the necessary resources to be successful. The case managers may authorize equipment, supplies, and incidental goods and services to ensure the

---

(...continued)

chapter 33; Chapters 106a, 1606, and 1607 of Title 10 U.S.C.; Section 903 of the Department of Defense Authorization Act, 1981 (10 U.S.C. 2141 note); the Hostage Relief Act of 1980 (5 U.S.C. 5561 note); and the Omnibus Diplomatic Security and Antiterrorism Act of 1986 (22 U.S.C. 4801).

[61] 38 C.F.R. §21.9750(m).

[62] As enacted by the Honoring America's Veterans and Caring for Camp Lejeune Families Act of 2012 (P.L. 112-154), the allowance of 81 months of entitlement applies only to entitlement that was not exhausted prior to October 1, 2013.

[63] For more detailed information on the VR&E program, see CRS Report RL34627, *Veterans' Benefits: The Vocational Rehabilitation and Employment Program*, by Benjamin Collins.

[64] This provision went into effect August 1, 2011, as a consequence of the Improvements Act.

[65] For an in-depth discussion of the VA's disability evaluation process and policies, see CRS Report RL33991, *Disability Evaluation of Military Servicemembers*, by Christine Scott and Don J. Jansen.

---

veterans' success as long as the cost of the incidental goods and services does not exceed 5% of the annual training cost. After successful completion of the individualized rehabilitation plan, veterans may be eligible to receive two additional months of the subsistence allowance while receiving employment placement services.

Participation and Cost

The Post-9/11 GI Bill is an *appropriated entitlement* program, meaning the entitlement spending is funded in annual appropriations acts. While the funding is provided in the annual appropriations acts, the level of spending for appropriated entitlements is not controlled through the annual appropriations process. Instead, the level of spending for appropriated entitlements is based on the benefit and eligibility criteria established in law, and the amount provided in appropriations acts is based on meeting this projected level.

Obligations for the Post-9/11 GI Bill increased from $5.5 billion in FY2010, the first full year of implementation, to $10.2 billion in FY2013 (**Table 3**). Participation exceeded 350,000 in FY2010 and exceeded 750,000 in FY2013. In FY2010, participants received over $14,000 in benefits, on average, and in FY2013, participants received over $13,000 in benefits, on average. Participation data by program of education is not currently available.

Table 3. Post-9/11 GI Bill Obligations, Participation, and Benefit Amount per Participant: FY2009-FY2013

Fiscal Year	Obligations ($ in thousands)	Participation[a]	Average Benefit per Participant ($)
2009[b]	162,053	34,393	4,712
2010	5,542,843	365,640	14,466
2011	7,656,490	555,329	13,871
2012	8,476,227	646,302	13,080
2013	10,184,499	754,529	13,465

Source: President's Budget Submission, FY2011-FY2015.

a. Participants include veterans, servicemembers, and dependents. Participants may receive benefits in more than one year and from more than one program in the same year.

b. Since the program went into effect on August 1, 2009, one month before the end of FY2009, the data do not reflect the full year.

Key Issues

FY2011 participation in the Post-9/11 GI Bill exceeded the annual participation in all of the other GI Bills since 1984. The Post-9/11 GI Bill average per participant benefit in FY2013 ($13,465) was higher than that of the MGIB-AD ($8,551), the GI Bill with the next highest participation and obligations. The large number of participants and the fact that the benefit level is higher than the MGIB-AD have focused attention on several program issues. A few of the issues are described below.

Benefits for Out-of-State (In-State) Tuition and Fees

Some Post-9/11 GI Bill participants have suggested that the tuition and fees payment amount for out-of-state tuition and fees is inequitable when compared to the payment amount for in-state tuition and fees and when compared to tuition and fees at private IHLs. The tuition and fees payment covers all of the tuition and fees charges for participants at the 100% benefit level attending public IHLs *in-state*. The maximum tuition and fees payment at private IHLs exceeds undergraduate in-state tuition and fees at the overwhelming majority of public IHLs. Participants at the 100% benefit level attending public IHLs out-of-state may incur a considerable out-of-pocket cost if the Yellow Ribbon program does not make up the difference.

Currently, participants at the 100% benefit level attending public IHLs are eligible for up to the full cost of *in-state* tuition and fees. In academic year (AY) 2011-2012, average tuition and fees at four-year public institutions of higher education (IHEs)[66] were $7,234 for in-state students and $16,457 (more than double) for out-of-state students.[67] At two-year public IHEs in AY2011-2012, average tuition and fees were $3,384 for in-state students and $6,888 (more than double) for out-of-state students.[68] Therefore, on average, individuals enrolled full-time in public IHLs as out-of-state students could potentially have had a substantial out-of-pocket cost. The difference in the averages of the in-state and out-of-state tuition and fees levels is $9,223 at a four-year public IHL and $3,504 at a two-year public IHL.

At private IHLs in AY2011-2012, most Post-9/11 GI Bill participants at the 100% benefit level were eligible for up to $17,500 for tuition and fees. AY2011-2012 average undergraduate tuition and fees were $23,343 at four-year private nonprofit IHEs, $15,234 at four-year private for-profit IHEs, $13,204 at two-year private nonprofit IHEs, and $14,131 at two-year private for-profit IHEs.[69] Individuals enrolled full-time in private nonprofit IHLs could potentially have had a sizable out-of-pocket cost. The difference in the average tuition and fees levels and $17,500 is $5,843 at four-year private nonprofit IHEs. Whereas, individuals at the 100% benefit level enrolled in other institutional sectors could potentially have no out-of-pocket costs.

Therefore, the potential out-of-pocket costs for individuals attending out-of-state public IHLs are considered by some to be inequitable for three main reasons:

- Prior to the Improvements Act, many individuals attending lower-cost public IHLs out-of-state received a higher tuition and fees payment since the maximum tuition and fees payment was equal to the maximum amount of undergraduate in-state tuition and fees charged in the state.

---

[66] The term, institution of higher education (IHE), is defined in Sections 101 and 102 of the Higher Education Act of 1965 (HEA), as amended. An IHE admits as regular students only those who have a high school diploma or its equivalent or who are beyond the age of compulsory school attendance. An IHE must be legally authorized by the state and must be accredited by an accrediting agency recognized by ED. IHEs include less-than-two-year, two-year, and four-year institutions.

[67] L.G. Knapp, J.E. Kelly-Reid, and S.A. Ginder, Postsecondary Institutions and Price of Attendance in 2011-12, Degrees and Other Awards Conferred: 2010-11, and 12-Month Enrollment: 2010-11 (NCES 2012-289), U.S. Department of Education, Washington, DC: National Center for Education Statistics, 2012, p. 5. Retrieved September 10, 2012, from http://nces.ed.gov/pubsearch.

[68] Ibid.

[69] Ibid.

- Since the Post-9/11 GI Bill was intended to pay a significant portion of each individual's education, providing a higher tuition and fees payment to some individuals at the same benefit level and program of education does not seem equitable to some participants.

- The difference in potential out-of-pocket costs for individuals attending out-of-state public IHLs and individuals attending private IHLs is viewed as inequitable by some participants.

Potential options have been posited to resolve the issue, and several bills have been introduced and considered in the 113th Congress to address the issue.[70] One concern is whether the issue should be addressed for all veterans, Post-9/11 GI Bill participants, all GI Bill participants, or some subset. Some states have passed legislation allowing individuals who have been recently discharged or retired from the military to pay in-state tuition and fees. Congress could amend the Higher Education Act (HEA) or Title 38 of the U.S. Code to require that states charge veterans and their family members in-state tuition and fees, but this would impose costs on the state or institution. Congress amended the HEA in 2008 to require states to provide members of the Armed Forces on active duty, their spouses, and their dependent children with in-state tuition at public institutions if they are domiciled or stationed on permanent duty within the state for more than 30 days. Alternatively, should Congress opt to address this, the Post-9/11 GI Bill could be amended to provide a tuition and fees benefit for individuals charged out-of-state tuition and fees of (1) up to out-of-state tuition and fees or (2) up to the maximum amount allowable for individuals attending private IHLs. Also, the Post-9/11 GI Bill could be amended to provide a single maximum tuition and fees benefit regardless of institution and level of education.

Quality of Programs of Education

The quality of the programs of education and educational institutions at which GI Bill participants use their benefits has been raised as an issue for various reasons. One reason is the belief that the federal government should be accountable for the use of taxpayer funds. Another reason is that supporting enrollment in poor quality programs is not consistent with a goal of helping ensure that the nation's veterans and servicemembers have a real opportunity for success in their civilian lives. Finally, during the 112th and 113th Congresses, the Senate Health, Education, Labor, and Pensions Committee, chaired by Senator Harkin, has focused attention more generally on the quality of education provided by some for-profit IHEs to individuals receiving federal funds for education.

Participant Educational and Employment Outcomes

Three potential measures of educational quality are the extent to which individuals achieve their educational or career objective, complete the program of education, or achieve related

---

[70] Different versions of the Veterans' Access to Care through Choice, Accountability, and Transparency Act of 2014 (H.R. 3230) passed the House on October 3, 2013, and Senate on June 11, 2014. The GI Bill Tuition Fairness Act of 2013 (H.R. 357 and S. 257) passed the House on February 3, 2014. The Veterans Health and Benefits Improvement Act of 2013 (S. 944) was approved by the Senate Committee on Veterans' Affairs on December 9, 2013. The Veterans Education Equity Act of 2013 (H.R. 595 and S. 262) and Comprehensive Veterans Health and Benefits and Military Retirement Pay Restoration Act of 2014 (S. 1982) were introduced in the 113th Congress.

---

employment. Of course, dynamics other than educational quality such as personal motivation and the health of the overall economy also factor into the measures.

Data on GI Bill participants' program completions and employment outcomes have not been consistently collected. In 1974, the GAO surveyed 15,000 individuals who participated in the Post-Korea and Vietnam Era GI Bill.[71] The survey indicated that, of the individuals who began using their benefit in 1968, 92% completed their apprenticeship, 59% completed their vocational/technical program, and 72% completed an undergraduate program while enrolled full-time. Of all participants who had completed their program, 89% of those from apprentices, 43% from vocational/technical programs, and 44% from undergraduate programs were employed in the same type of work for which they trained.

A 2003 Program Assessment Rating Tool review of the MGIB by the Office of Management and Budget (OMB) recommended that the VA establish an outcome measure regarding veterans' readjustment to civilian life. As a consequence, VA indicated that it planned to have degree attainment data by 2009. The VA FY2009 Annual Benefits Report indicated that 29% of the MGIB-AD, MGIB-SR, and REAP beneficiaries found in the National Student Clearinghouse (NSC) had completed a degree or certificate. The NSC, a nonprofit organization founded by the higher education community, collects enrollment and degree records from more than 3,600 colleges and universities that enroll 98% of all students in public and private U.S. institutions.

The 2010 *National Survey of Veterans* indicated that of veterans who were receiving VA education and training benefits, 66.6% of them completed the training or received the degree or certificate in which they were enrolled.[72]

Most recently, the Student Veterans of America (SVA) partnered with the VA and NSC to report educational outcomes of individuals who used the MGIB, Post-9/11 GI Bill, or both between 2002 and 2010. The report was based on a VA-generated random sample of veterans who attended institutions that were known to report data to the NSC. The sample included 500,000 individuals who first used the MGIB between 2002 and 2010 and 500,000 individuals who first used the Post-9/11 GI Bill between 2009 and 2010. Of the 1 million individuals, outcome data on 788,915 were available for the final analysis.[73] As of spring 2013, NSC data indicated that 51.7% had earned a postsecondary education credential (certificate or degree).[74] Although the analysis reports the number of participants who earned a credential between 2002 and 2010, a major limitation is that it does not distinguish individuals who earned the credential before, during, or after using the GI Bill.[75]

---

[71] U.S. General Accounting Office (now called the Government Accountability Office), *Veterans' Responses to GAO Questionnaires on the Operation and Effect of VA Educational Assistance Programs Under 38 U.S.C. 1651 et. se.*, B-114859, August 11, 1976.

[72] Westat, *National Survey of Veterans, Active Duty Service Members, Demobilized National Guard and Reserve Members, Family Members, and Surviving Spouses*, Department of Veterans, Washington, DC, October 18, 2010, p. 146.

[73] The NSC found data for 859,297. An additional 70,382 individuals were excluded because their earliest initial postsecondary enrollment date was January 1, 2011, or later.

[74] Only 75% of the educational institutions had reported completions for spring 2013.

[75] C.A. Cate, *Million Records Project: Research from Student Veterans of America*, Student Veterans of America, Washington, DC, 2014.

In summer 2011, the VA announced that it was beginning to collect data on "veterans' programs of study, veterans on academic probation and those terminated for unsatisfactory progress, and veterans' graduation rates."[76] In the July 2, 2012, Federal Register, the VA announced its intention to collect survey data on individuals who began participating in the Post 9/11-GI Bill during FY2010, FY2012, and FY2014 to determine the long-term positive outcomes of participants.[77] The purpose of this study is to assess the effectiveness of the Post 9/11-GI Bill. Results of the data collection have not been published.

The Honoring America's Veterans and Caring for Camp Lejeune Families Act of 2012 requires the Secretary of Defense to report to Congress on the Post-9/11 GI Bill and requires the Secretary of Veterans Affairs to report to Congress on the Post-9/11 GI Bill and the DEA. The reports are due annually, starting no later than November 13, 2013, through January 1, 2021. The Defense report must include the extent to which Post-9/11 GI Bill benefit levels affect recruitment to and retention in the Armed Forces, the extent to which the benefits help meet the cost of pursuing a program of education, the necessity of the benefits for future recruitment to the active duty service, the results from and efforts to inform members of the Armed Forces of the active duty eligibility requirements, and recommendations for administrative and legislative changes. The Veterans Affairs report must include information on the extent to which Post-9/11 GI Bill and DEA benefits are used, program expenditures, student outcome measures, and recommendations for administrative and legislative changes.

Overall, however, limited data are available on participant educational and employment outcomes.

Counseling and Informational Services

Some stakeholders have suggested that servicemembers and veterans are not sufficiently informed about their GI Bill benefits, higher education, and civilian employment opportunities to make the best decisions regarding the use of GI Bill benefits. Although the VA does provide access to academic and career counseling, it does not provide information on being a savvy consumer of higher education. In addition, some veterans need assistance negotiating education while recovering or dealing with the impacts of traumatic brain injury (TBI) or post-traumatic stress disorder (PTSD).

If requested, the VA provides academic and career counseling to individuals within six months of discharge from active duty or within one year following discharge from active duty under other than dishonorable conditions. The academic and career counseling includes help making career decisions; the development of an appropriate training or educational program; and the resolution of barriers to success in education, training, and employment. Some stakeholders have suggested that all GI Bill participants need to receive academic and career counseling.

Under the VA VetSuccess on Campus (VSOC) program, a full-time, experienced VR&E counselor and a part-time Vet Center Outreach Coordinator from the VA are assigned a campus to provide VA benefits outreach, support, and assistance to ensure the health, educational, and

---

[76] Secretary Eric K. Shinseki, "Student Veterans of America, 4th Annual Convention," University of Wisconsin, June 3, 2011, http://www.va.gov/opa/speeches/2011/06_06_2011_student_veterans_america.asp.

[77] Veterans Benefits Administration, Department of Veterans Affairs, "Agency Information (Post-9/11 GI Bill Education Longitudinal Study Survey) Activity Under OMB Review," 77 *Federal Register* 39344, July 2, 2012.

benefit needs of campus veterans are met. VA conducts outreach activities through direct emails, posters, social media posts, articles in campus newspapers, campus website links, and outreach events at the student commons. The VSOC program began in June 2009 as a pilot project at the University of South Florida. In 2014 and 2015, VetSuccess on Campus will be operational at 94 campuses.

Executive Order 13607, *Establishing Principles of Excellence for Educational Institutions Serving Service Members, Veterans, Spouses, and Other Family Members*, signed April 27, 2012, was intended to help veterans and servicemembers and their families make more informed decisions about their benefits. The Executive Order encourages educational institutions receiving veterans and military educational benefits, to the extent permitted by law, to abide by the *Principles of Excellence*. The principles encourage educational institutions to

- "provide meaningful information to service members, veterans, spouses, and other family members about [the institution's] financial cost and quality";

- end fraudulent and aggressive recruiting;

- gain accreditation for new programs of education before enrolling students;

- provide high quality academic and student support services;

- provide a timeline and education plan for graduation; and

- designate a point-of-contact for academic and financial advising and career services.[78]

The order further requires the VA, DOD, and Department of Education (ED) to develop consistent student outcome measures; requires the VA to provide tools to help students use their benefits; and requires the VA and DOD to implement a centralized complaint system.

The principle of ensuring better informed and protected GI Bill participants, as intended by Executive Order 13607, was furthered by enactment of the Improving Transparency of Education Opportunities for Veterans Act of 2012 (P.L. 112-249) on January 10, 2013. The bill requires the VA to develop a comprehensive policy to improve outreach and transparency to veterans and servicemembers, among other purposes. The policy must include several elements including, but not limited to, outreach about available counseling, a system of student feedback on IHL experiences and outcomes, information sharing between State Approving Agencies and Department of Education recognized accrediting agencies,[79] and information about relevant postsecondary education and training opportunities.

Several initiatives have resulted from the executive order and P.L. 112-249. In November 2012, the VA provided a link on the GI Bill website to ED's College Navigator, which provides institutional information, including enrollment, programs, and cost. In August 2013, President Obama announced the 8 Keys to Success, which guide educational institutions in helping veterans

---

[78] Executive Order 13607, "Establishing Principles of Excellence for Educational Institutions Serving Service Members, Veterans, Spouses, and Other Family Members," 77 *Federal Register* 25861-25864, May 2, 2012.

[79] The VA funds State Approving Agencies to approve and review the quality of programs of education for use with GI Bill benefits. The U.S. Department of Education recognizes accrediting agencies to help ensure a level of acceptable quality across programs and institutions of higher education at which benefits authorized by Title IV of the Higher Education Act may be used.

and servicemembers transition to the classroom. In January 2014, the VA opened the GI Bill Feedback System that acts as a centralized complaint system through which it initiates resolution.[80] In February 2014, the VA launched the Comparison Tool/GI Bill Benefit Estimator that helps prospective students calculate benefits and research approved programs.[81] Also in 2014, the VA made CareerScope available so individuals can assess their aptitudes and interests in relation to careers.[82]

Relationship to Department of Education Student Financial Aid Programs

Although statutory provisions limit the amount of educational assistance received by educational institutions from the VA and ED separately, statutory provisions do not limit the combined amount of educational assistance. This has resulted in concerns that some poor quality educational institutions have recruited GI Bill participants to maintain access to a portion of the $217 billion in ED grants, loans, and work-study assistance provided to help students pay for postsecondary education in FY2012.

Under the GI Bills, individuals may not receive benefits for enrollment in courses in which more than 85% of the students enrolled in the course are having all or part of their tuition, fees, or other charges paid to or for them by the educational institution or by the VA. This restriction does not apply if (1) waived by Secretary, (2) the total GI Bill participant enrollment in the institution is less than or equal to 35%, or (3) the course is offered under contract to the DOD or the Coast Guard and is given on or near a military installation/facility.

Under the ED-administered federal student aid programs authorized by Title IV of the Higher Education Act (HEA), a private for-profit IHE must derive at least 10% of its total revenue from non-Title IV funds (or conversely, no more than 90% of its revenue from Title IV funds) during a fiscal year. The 10% requirement, as specified in law, forms the basis for the so-called "90/10 rule."

Several bills were introduced in the 112th and 113th Congresses to amend the 90/10 rule to limit revenue from Title IV, GI Bill, and other federal funds to no more than 90% for private for-profit IHEs.[83] A 1997 report by the Government Accountability Office (GAO) indicated that decreasing the limit on Title IV funds to 45% could reduce Title IV student loan default rates—a presumed indicator of educational quality.[84] At the same time, the GAO and opponents of changing the 90/10 rule have noted that revisions could reduce access to postsecondary education for disadvantaged populations, in particular.

---

[80] http://www.benefits.va.gov/GIBILL/Feedback.asp.

[81] http://department-of-veterans-affairs.github.io/gi-bill-comparison-tool/.

[82] http://www.benefits.va.gov/gibill/careerscope.asp.

[83] The Ensuring Quality Education for Veterans Act (H.R. 3764); Military and Veterans Education Protection Act (S. 2116 and H.R. 4055); POST Act (S. 2032); and Veterans and Service Members Educational Benefits Safety Act (H.R. 5836) were introduced in the 112th Congress. The POST Act of 2013 (H.R. 3496) was introduced in the 113th Congress.

[84] U.S. General Accounting Office, *Proprietary Schools: Poorer Student Outcomes at Schools that Rely More on Federal Student Aid*, GAO/HEHS-97-103, June 13, 1997.

Recovery of Overpayments

Post-9/11 GI Bill participants and educational institutions have focused some attention on the perceived problems and confusion over how the VA assigns liability for overpayments and the collection process.[85] An overpayment occurs when the VA processes a payment that exceeds the amount to which an individual is entitled. Depending on the nature of the overpayment, either the GI Bill participant or the educational institution may be liable for the overpayment.[86] Overpayments most often occur when participants decrease their enrollment rate. Repaying overpayments creates a financial burden on participants, and outstanding overpayments may affect the participants' credit rating.

When the VA uncovers overpayments, an explanation of the debt and amount is sent to the individuals and/or the educational institutions. Individuals must contact the VA's Debt Management Center (DMC) to repay the debt, establish a repayment plan, dispute the debt, or request a waiver of debt. In April 2011, the VA allowed Post-9/11 GI Bill participants to repay debts over a one-year period rather than by the end of the academic term as was previously required.[87] If individuals do not resolve the debt in a timely manner, the debt may be reported to credit reporting agencies, transferred to the Department of the Treasury for collection, and referred to private collection agencies.

Besides the personal liability of individuals for overpayments, two additional issues have been raised. A portion of the tuition and fees overpayments may be refunded to the participants (or the VA) by the educational institutions according to the institutions' policy. The institutions' refund amount may be less than the VA's calculated overpayment amount, leaving individuals with outstanding debt. Depending on the timing for educational institutions to certify to the VA that individuals have reduced their enrollment rate, multiple months of the housing allowance may have been overpaid.

Several potential options have been posited to resolve the issue. Tuition and fees payments are often the cause of the largest overpayments. The VA could provide tuition and fee payments directly to participants instead of educational institutions to reduce some confusion regarding liability. The VA could delay payment until it is less likely that an individual would change her enrollment status, that is, after the drop date, halfway through an academic term, or at the end of the academic term. Alternatively, the VA could disburse the total tuition and fees payment over multiple installments throughout the academic term. In the case of students who change their enrollment rate, the amount of the GI Bill tuition and fees overpayment could be limited to the amount of any tuition and fees refund from the educational institution. Tuition and fees overpayments that are not the result of a participant's willful misconduct or deception could become the liability of the educational institution, requiring the educational institution to recoup funds from the student. The VA could lengthen the time before reporting the debt to credit reporting agencies. The VA could also extend the length of time over which an individual must

---

[85] U.S. Congress, House Committee on Veterans' Affairs, Subcommittee on Economic Opportunity, *Update of the Post-9/11 GI Bill*, 111th Cong., 2nd sess., September 16, 2010, H.Hrg. 111-99 (Washington: GPO, 2011).

[86] Post-9/11 GI Bill participants are not liable for overpayments that result from an administrative error by the federal government. IHLs are liable for overpayments made to the IHL if the Post-9/11 GI Bill participant failed to attend or the overpayment is the result of the IHL's willful or negligent error, failure to report in a timely manner, or error.

[87] Rick Maze, "VA extends Post-9/11 GI Bill overpayment period," *ArmyTimes*, June 2, 2011.

repay the overpayment. Conversely, the VA could reduce the individual's entitlement until or unless the debt is collected.

Transferability for Former Servicemembers

The inability of former servicemembers, those who retired or were discharged or released prior to August 1, 2009, to transfer their Post-9/11 GI Bill benefits has been raised as an inequity. The transferability benefit was largely included in the Post-9/11 GI Bill at the request of the DOD to encourage the retention of individuals in the Armed Forces. There was concern that the liberal benefit would encourage individuals to leave the military in order to pursue education. Transferred benefits are also more expensive to the federal government than servicemembers and veterans using their own benefit. A transferability provision was removed from early draft versions of the MGIB-AD, enacted in 1985, in order to reduce cost.

By law, a Post-9/11 GI Bill-eligible individual "may transfer such entitlement only while serving as a member of the Armed Forces when the transfer is executed." Also, in order to designate the transfer of Post-9/11 GI Bill benefits to a dependent, an individual must have completed six years of service in the Armed Forces and agree to serve at least four additional years or the amount of time regulated by DOD.[88] Therefore, retirees and former servicemembers are ineligible to transfer their benefits.

Benefits for Business Start-Ups and Entrepreneurs

For several years, some of the veterans service organizations (VSOs) have advocated for the ability of GI Bill participants to use their benefits to start a business. GI Bill benefits may generally be used for education and training to help individuals prepare to start a business. Specifically, the benefits may be used for

- courses offered by a qualified provider of entrepreneurship courses;

- courses required by the Administrator of the Small Business Administration (SBA) as a condition for obtaining financial assistance under the provisions of Section 7(i)(1) of the Small Business Act (15 U.S.C. 636(i)(1)); and

- self-employment on-the-job training consisting of full-time training for a period of less than six months that is needed or accepted for purposes of obtaining licensure to engage in a self-employment occupation or required for ownership and operation of a franchise that is the objective of the training.

GI Bill benefits, however, may not be used for business start-up costs or franchise fees.

GI Bill benefits are a readjustment benefit to help veterans join the civilian workforce. Some of the VSOs contend that entrepreneurship and starting a business is one way to join the civilian workforce. Opponents believe that the SBA has adequate programs in this regard and that evaluating business plans may be outside the VA's expertise.

---

[88] Regulations have limited the 10-year obligation to service in the active duty and/or Selected Reserve (Source: Office of the Under Secretary of Defense, *Directive-Type Memorandum (DTM) 09-003: Post-9/11 GI Bill*, June 22, 2009, Incorporating Change 2, September 14, 2011).

Qualifying Active Duty

In *The Eleventh Quadrennial Review of Military Compensation*, DOD noted inequities in the types of active duty that qualify for the Post-9/11 GI Bill.[89] Some involuntary and voluntary service by members of the guard and reserve that is similar to current qualifying active service does not qualify, including new activation authorities. DOD recommends expanding the definition of qualifying active duty service to include

- voluntary orders for authorized health care by reservists (10 U.S.C. §12301(h));

- involuntary orders to respond to major disasters or emergencies by reservists (10 U.S.C. §12304a);

- involuntary orders by reservists for preplanned missions in support of combatant commands (10 U.S.C. §12304b);

- voluntary orders to receive treatment for or recover from an injury or illness incurred or aggravated while performing inactive duty ("drill") for more than 30 days by reservists (10 U.S.C. §12322);

- involuntary orders to respond full-time to major disasters or emergencies by National Guard members under the command of the governor (32 U.S.C. §501(f)(1)(A));

- voluntary orders by National Guard members to perform DOD missions, such as drug interdiction and counter drug activities, or to maintain programs, such as the National Guard youth challenge program (32 U.S.C. §502(f)); and

- voluntary orders by National Guard members at the request of the president under the command of the governor to assist federal agencies when the country is not under a national emergency and when the national emergency does not cover the duty's purpose (Title 32 of the U.S. Code).

Author Contact Information

Cassandria Dortch
Analyst in Education Policy
cdortch@crs.loc.gov, 7-0376

---

[89] Department of Defense, *Report of the Eleventh Annual Quadrennial Review of Military Compensation*, June 2012, pp. 199-201.